Breaking their Chains:
Mary Macarthur and the
Chainmakers' Strike of 1910

Tony Barnsley

D1556075

BREAKING THEIR CHAINS

Mary Macarthur and the Chainmakers' Strike of 1910

Tony Barnsley

Bookmarks *Publications*

Breaking their Chains:
Mary Macarthur and the Chainmakers' Strike of 1910

Tony Barnsley

First published in July 2010 by Bookmarks Publications
This edition printed July 2011
c/o 1 Bloomsbury Street, London WC1B 3QE
© Bookmarks Publications

Cover photohgraph: Mary Macarthur agitating among a crowd in
Cradley Heath—Black Country Living Museum, Dudley
Typeset by Bookmarks Publications
Printed by Halstan Printing Group

ISBN 978 1905 192 649

CONTENTS

Acknowledgements

Thanks for the political input from *Socialist Worker* comrades Pete Jackson and Helen Salmon. Thanks also to Sally Campbell from Bookmarks. Thanks to Barbara Harris of the Black Country Living Museum and to all the helpful workers at both Dudley and Sandwell Archive Services. For copies of the pictures thanks go to the Black Country Living Museum, *Stourbridge News*, the TUC and Sandwell MBC's Archive Service.

But the biggest thanks go to Christina, Leon, Zac and Martha for their support and understanding in providing the space and time to write.

INTRODUCTION

For two months in the autumn of 1910 hundreds of women chain makers in the Black Country struck against their employers and won a minimum wage which doubled their incomes. Women who had no vote, who were largely illiterate, who worked 54-hour weeks for a pittance and had to take their children to work with them took on their bosses and proved their economic power.

But more than this, the women chain makers of Cradley Heath returned to work confident in the knowledge that by sticking together in a union they could stand up to the chain masters. Delegations of strikers had visited places they had never been to before. They had seen more daylight than ever before. They experienced being at the centre of press interest, had been interviewed for the first time and perhaps photographed for the first time.

The events of the first day of the strike were witnessed by the novelist John Galsworthy (author of *The Forsythe Saga*), who happened to be in Cradley Heath. Galsworthy described the spirit and joy of the women when they began their strike. After working since 7am the forges of Cradley all stood still at 2pm. He described how the sun broke through the usually smoky air, and 1,000 women and children marched through the streets, faces full of the joy of rebellion, waving flags, chanting and laughing:

> For an hour the pageant wound through the dejected street...till it came to a deserted slag heap, selected for speech making...as I watched, a strong fancy visited my brain. I

seemed to see over every rugged head of these marching women a little yellow flame, a thin flickering gleam…a trick of the sunlight maybe? Or was it the life in their heads, the indistinguishable breath of happiness had for a moment escaped prison, and was fluttering at the pleasure of the breeze?…

It seemed to me that in these tattered, wistful figures, so still, so trustful, I was looking on such beauty as I had never beheld.

The women chain makers' strike of 1910 is a slice of British working class history that until recently had largely been forgotten.

Such was the support for the chain makers' strike at the time that not only was there enough money for strike pay, but there was enough left over to build the Workers' Institute in Cradley Heath.

It was the decision to demolish the Workers' Institute to make way for a new road and superstore that stirred local memory of the struggle.

To ensure this piece of working class history was not lost, the Black Country Living Museum has since rebuilt the Workers' Institute and has held an annual festival commemorating the achievements of the strike.

"The history of all hitherto existing society is the history of class struggles," Karl Marx succinctly wrote. History is marked by wars, revolutions and struggles. Often history is told purely through the eyes of the victorious rulers as though such events simply happen to us, ignoring the role ordinary people play in making the world.

This book is written with the view that people make history. But to fully appreciate the significance of any struggle it is necessary to place it in its social and historical context.

Therefore the book begins by examining the social and political conditions of an industrialising Britain and the specific industrial development of the Black Country, which Cradley Heath is a part of.

While there are many differences between the social conditions of early industrialisation and Cradley Heath in 1910 and Britain today, there are also some striking similarities.

The women chain makers' strike of 1910 is a strike in which the most downtrodden, exploited and unorganised workers took on their masters and middlemen and achieved a resounding victory.

I hope this book adds to the collective memory of this strike but also informs today's workers and trade unionists what needs to be done in order to win the struggles and strikes of today and tomorrow.

Finally I hope this work helps to rediscover the huge contribution trade union organiser Mary Macarthur made to both the labour movement and the struggle for equality, not just between men and women, but also between classes.

Tony Barnsley
27 October 2009

1.

LIFE IN EARLY INDUSTRIAL BRITAIN

By 1910 the process of urbanisation and the creation of industrial towns such as Cradley Heath and the wider Black Country had been ongoing for around 150 years.

The Industrial Revolution brought great change to Britain over this period. From being a largely agricultural society Britain had been transformed into a country where the majority of people lived in towns and cities. In 1750 just 17.5 percent of England's population lived in towns with more than 10,000 people. By 1840 this had increased to 48 percent.

There was a rapid expansion in the population of Britain. The number of people living in England in 1751 was around 6 million. By 1851 it had grown to around 17 million.[1] This expansion continued throughout the 19th century with the Census of 1911 showing Britain to have a population of 45 million.

This population growth and process of urbanisation meant that by 1901 around 78 percent of the population lived in towns. The number of towns with 50,000 or more inhabitants doubled in just 30 years. Over half of all towns of 50,000 plus were located on or near coalfields. Another third were coastal port towns such as Liverpool and Hull.

London's population had grown from 3.9 million in 1871 to 7.2 million by 1911. The West Midlands grew from just under 1 million to 1.6 million during this period.

Unlike today, there were concerns in 1910 that population growth had begun to decline. Between 1901 and 1910 the number of people emigrating from the country rose from 284,000 to 464,000 each year.[2] With the people migrating usually being young and healthy, the concern was that there would not be enough fit young workers to undertake all the work in the factories, mines and ports in Britain.

To understand this concern it is important to recognise just how quickly the economy expanded during early industrialisation. Taking 1780 to represent an industrial production index of 100, by 1830—just 50 years later— the index was 361.[3] And although there were periodic slumps and recessions the economy continued to grow significantly throughout the 19th century.

This is an era before the development of the welfare state and social security. People moved together geographically out of the need to find work in order to eat and live. Every modern town is a product of migration.

There was nothing planned about this great movement of people. The towns developed in a chaotic manner. Factories, mines and mills were located where the industrial capitalists could make a profit. Workers followed or faced the prospect of starvation.

Housing

Wherever migrant workers came from they had to find a home in the new towns. Having no money most had little choice but to either rent rooms or small homes, sometimes directly from their employers.

While industrial expansion created huge wealth and profits for the new capitalists, it also created huge misery and squalor.

The rich lived in luxurious stately homes, many of which are today owned by such institutions as the National Trust. There are many works of literature and TV period dramas that portray the splendour of Victorian Britain. Yet the Capability Brown landscaped gardens are a sharp contrast to the small brick back-yard that the majority of workers would have had.

Most lived in cramp, cold, damp terraces. Toilet facilities would be shared by many outside. Water supplies often got contaminated and diseases such as cholera and typhoid were common.

One of the best early pieces of work that documented the social conditions endured by the working class was written by the socialist and friend to Karl Marx, Frederick Engels. Written in 1845, *The Condition of the Working Class in England* gives a clear picture:

> The most extensive working people's district lies east of the Tower [of London] in Whitechapel and Bethnal Green, where the greatest masses of London working people live. Let us hear M G Alston, preacher of St Phillip's, Bethnal Green, on the condition of his parish. He says:
>
> "It contains 1,400 houses, inhabited by 2,795 families, or about 12,000 persons. The space upon which this large population dwells is less than 400 yards square, and in this overcrowding it is nothing unusual to find a man, his wife, four or five children, and, sometimes, both grandparents, all in one single room of ten or twelve square feet, where they eat, sleep and work... And if we make ourselves acquainted with these unfortunates, through personal observation, if we watch them at their scanty meal and see them bowed by illness and want of work, we shall find such a mass of helplessness and misery, that a nation like ours must blush that these things can be possible."

And not everyone could achieve the squalor described above. To quote Engels, "In London 50,000 human beings get up every morning, not knowing where they are to lay their heads at night."

This level of poverty was not just restricted to London. Engels describes such conditions in several provincial towns:

In the other great seaport towns the prospect is no better. Liverpool, with all its commerce, wealth, and grandeur, yet treats its workers with the same barbarity. A full fifth of the population, more than 45,000 human beings, live in narrow, dark, damp, badly ventilated cellar dwellings, of which there are 7,862 in the city.

Engels was living in Manchester at the time and was therefore more familiar with this part of Britain than any other:

> If we briefly formulate the result of our wanderings, we must admit that 350,000 working people of Manchester and its environs live, almost all of them, in wretched, damp, filthy cottages, that the streets that surround them are usually in the most miserable and filthy condition, laid out without the slightest reference to ventilation, with reference solely to the profit secured by the contractor. In a word, we must confess that in the working men's dwellings of Manchester, no cleanliness, no convenience, and consequently no comfortable family life is possible.

By our modern Western standards these conditions would be totally unacceptable. However, it is striking that in parts of the world where industrialisation is new and expanding, such as India and China, there are no doubt many working class people suffering the same miserable conditions.

The workshop of the world
Despite periodic economic slumps capitalism in Britain and across the world continued to expand significantly during the second half of the 19th century. It is not the purpose of this book to chart this expansion in detail, however, it is worth noting that by the time of the women

chain makers' strike in 1910 the conditions for the vast majority of workers, while not great, were better than those described by Engels in 1845.

The period saw a number of campaigns, struggles, disputes and then acts of Parliament that firstly began to restrict the use of child labour and then working hours in general.

The more enlightened elements within the ruling and middle classes also realised that in order to stem the killer diseases of cholera and typhoid they needed to improve conditions in the slums.

The coal, iron, steel and shipbuilding industries boomed from 1850 onwards as capitalism began to spread across the world. In supplying the world with goods and the means to industrialise Britain became the "workshop of the world". There were huge profits to be made—so much so that employers were keen to avoid disruptions in much needed production and were therefore willing to concede to the wage demands of workers. It is estimated that average real wages rose by a third between 1850 and 1875.[4] From 1850 to 1910 national income almost quadrupled. Even with an expanding population the average income per head rose from £28 in 1873 to £50 in 1914.[5]

This was also a period of falling prices on many goods. One estimate puts the average increase in real wages between 1860 and 1900 at 60 percent.[6] Many workers could now afford housing and food far better than that described by Engels in 1845. However, while the average figures give an indication of the general trend they also hide some significant variations.

Inequality and class in Edwardian Britain
In Edwardian Britain the gap between rich and poor, already vast, grew even further. Although the economy and national income grew by a fifth between 1900 and

1913, real wages did not increase. In fact real wage rates in 1912-14 were lower than they were in 1900. Profit, in the form of dividends paid to shareholders, was taking an increasing share of the nation's wealth. In 1914 of all wealth bequeathed 90 percent was left by just 4 percent of those dying.[7]

The new industrial capitalists were accumulating huge amounts of wealth and joining the already rich landed aristocracy at the top of British class society.

There was also the development of a middle class in professional occupations—bank managers, solicitors, judges—who could secure wages well above those of the average worker.

The professional middle class not only had the benefit of large salaries and pensions but also a well defined place in the social hierarchy of the time. With low levels of taxation and a plentiful supply of cheap labour those earning a good income could afford to employ a number of domestic staff, as John Stevenson shows in his book, *British Society 1914-45*:

> A bank manager in Hertford earning £600 a year employed between 1897 and 1911 a housemaid at £12 to £16 a year and a cook at £16 to £20 a year, both of whom lived in; a "knife boy" paid at a shilling a day who cleaned knives and boots and shoes, chopped wood and brought coal for six or seven fires; a gardener employed once a week for between 2s 6d [two shillings and sixpence] and 4s 6d; and a live-in nursemaid or governess employed before the children were sent to boarding school.

In contrast the average male wage in 1906 was 27 shillings a week or £70 a year. Again this figure hides some alarming variations—for example between skilled and unskilled workers.

Workers earning above 27s a week had some margin of comfort and could afford a clean and decent home, feed and clothe a family and possibly even save a little. Those earning 20s a week (£1) had sufficient if they were single or a couple but not if they had children. A survey in 1904 of 2,000 working class households revealed that where households earned less than 25s a week 67 percent of their income would be used on buying basic food.

Another study in 1913, "Round About a Pound a Week", concluded that there were 2 million men, 8 million people including their families, who existed on under 25s a week. From a study of household budgets, the author Maud Pember Reeves stated:

> the great bulk of this enormous mass of people are underfed, under-housed, and insufficiently clothed. Their growth is stunted, their mental powers are cramped, their health is undermined.

Inequality, women and the vote

As well as class inequality there was also massive inequality between men and women.

Rich and middle class women were seen as the property of their husbands and fathers. Working class women earned significantly less than working class men. Just before the First World War, Sidney Webb estimated that average earnings for women stood at 10s 10d per week compared to an average of 25s 9d for men. Working class women were also expected to be the domestic slave in their household. And if that was not enough servitude then there was always the "prospect'" of being a servant for a wealthy household.

The sexist attitudes of the era are perhaps best high-lighted by the establishment's reluctance to allow women the vote.

The ruling class in Britain were scared to extend the vote to all working men, as the Chartists had demanded in the 1840s. They knew that the working class vastly outnumbered themselves and thought that if working class men could vote they would vote for workers' candidates, which would in turn threaten their wealth and power. The ruling class did gradually extend the vote to more men during the 19th century, but primarily men of property. The 1884 Reform Act meant 60 percent of men could vote, but the poorest 40 percent of men could not—and no women were allowed the vote, regardless of their wealth or social status.

Rich male politicians of the time argued against giving women the vote because they wanted to "keep control of them". The quote below is from the Tory MP for Colchester, E K Karslake, during a debate in 1867. He is arguing against John Stuart Mill's attempts to extend the franchise to women:

> A woman in marriage should give over all she has, including herself, to her husband for better, for worse. The wife should be absolutely and entirely under the control of her husband not only in respect of her property but of her personal movements. She may not "gad about", and if she does, her husband is entitled to lock her up. Some hold that he might beat her. I have my doubts about that and if my advice were asked as a lawyer, I would say "do not do it". But undoubtedly the husband has entire domain over the person and property of his wife.[8]

Such abhorrent views were common among the British ruling class and were used to justify the unequal treatment of women. Even some so-called radical Liberals of the era perpetuated such nonsense. Labouchere, a rich Eton-educated MP for Northampton, argued in the House of Commons in 1897:

I have always objected to petticoat government. I have always observed that ladies, for who I have the highest respect and admiration, are incapable of argument.[9]

The trade unions

Industrialisation destroyed the old craft methods of producing goods. Skilled craft workers could not compete against the new machinery and mass production of the factories and mills. Those whose livelihoods were immediately threatened reacted angrily. In several places organised groups of workers reacted by physically destroying the new machines. This movement, known as Luddism, was met with huge state repression. On one occasion 12,000 troops were sent to York to keep the Luddites in check.

However, once the new factories were established the Luddite method of destroying machinery meant destroying your own job and means to a livelihood.

With hundreds of thousands of people working in the same terrible conditions of early capitalist factories and mills, there was only one way of influencing the situation. Individuals could not challenge the might of their bosses. It was only by all workers in a workplace combining together as one, in a union, that workers could exert any pressure on their exploitative employers.

The early Combination Acts of 1799 and 1800 declared trade unions illegal, but in reality unions had already begun to form. In recognition of this the Combination Act of 1824 legalised trade unions but made picketing and other trade union tactics illegal.

The story of the British trade union movement is not one of smooth and rapid growth. Early attempts to build unions resulted in several hundred thousand being union members, but many factory owners and early industrialists tried to undermine any effective unions.

The most famous attempt to criminalise early trade unionists took place in Dorchester in 1834. Six agricultural labourers, known today as the Tolpuddle Martyrs, were transported to Australia. Their crime was swearing an oath to join a trade union.

However, the boom of the second half of the 19th century meant employers wanted to avoid disruption to production, and with increasing profits they could afford to make concessions to demands for improved wages and conditions. For example, in the cotton industry, where workers were unionised, the working day was reduced to just ten hours.

The early trade unionists tended to be skilled workers. It was not until the "New Unionism" movement at the end of the 19th century that unskilled workers were recruited to the militant unions that developed. Socialists such as Tom Mann saw the importance of strike action as the means of recruiting and achieving the aims of the trade union movement. Strikes in London's docks achieved better conditions for the dockers. Women workers too began to show signs of union organisation. In 1889 a specific women's trade union supported the strikes by the Bryant and May match girls, who won better pay and conditions.

While some in the labour movement sought to organise women workers, other trade unionists held some of the backward views of the ruling class and there was some reluctance to let women into certain trade unions and the Trades Union Congress.

In 1889 the growth of trade union activity led to 1,211 strikes involving 350,000 workers. Some of the strikes were for union recognition itself, some for better pay and some for the eight-hour day. Not every strike was successful, but the momentum was such that the gas workers' union, led by Will Thorne and Eleanor Marx, secured an agreement for an eight-hour day by the threat of strike action alone.

By 1900 trade union membership had increased to 2 million. However, the Taff Vale court ruling of 1901 made it easier for employers hit by strike action to sue the trade unions for any disruption to business. Trade unionists realised that they needed this legal ruling to be overturned if they were to continue to progress, and therefore the ruling had the impact of focusing trade unionists on political representation in parliament.

Up until then the trade unions had sought to influence Liberals into changing legislation. But the Liberals had increasingly failed to deliver the demands of the trade unions, who began to look towards the socialists within the ILP as the workers' representatives in parliament. The ILP had 26 MPs following the 1906 election and increased this further to 42 in 1910.

Although the Taff Vale decision was reversed in 1906, many other trade union demands were ignored by the Liberal government. Thus the need for trade unions to have their own representatives was increasingly recognised within the labour movement.

So when the women chain makers of Cradley Heath went on strike in 1910 it must be acknowledged that many workers had achieved some betterment upon the conditions most faced 50 years earlier. But also there was still huge inequality between the rich and poor; discrimination against women was legally enforced; women, on average, were paid less than half the wages of men; no women could vote and the dominant view was that women were not worthy of the vote; and that trade unions had grown but were still not huge in number. However, leading trade unionists had by then realised the importance of having a political voice, rather than facing the eternal prospect of being ruled by either overtly anti-trade union Conservatives or lukewarm unreliable Liberals.

2.

THE BLACK COUNTRY

The Black Country is an industrial area to the north west of Birmingham, with its own characteristics and dialect. It lies within the four modern day metropolitan boroughs of Dudley, Sandwell, Wolverhampton and Walsall, but would not include the whole of these boroughs.

The name "Black Country" came about during the industrial revolution, aptly describing the impact of industrialisation upon the area. The shallow nature of the coal seam under the Black Country, and the subsequent pits and furnaces of early industry meant that not only was the landscape scarred with the blackness from the pits and slag heaps, but also the air was often choked in a thick black smoke.

The abundance of minerals and coal at shallow depths made the Black Country a perfect place for industrialisation to take off. The development of smelting iron ore using coal instead of the more expensive charcoal meant that it became more economical to smelt iron where the coal existed. The transport network had already been established with the construction of canals. The Staffordshire and Worcestershire Canal, built between 1766 and 1772, linked the Severn and Trent rivers, initially to transport goods from the Potteries. With an additional branch cut between Wolverhampton and Birmingham it meant any minerals or goods from the Black Country could also be transported to wider markets.

Seeking to exploit these factors for industrial development was the then Lord Dudley of the Dudley Estate, which covered a significant part of the Black Country. Lord Dudley had access to parliament and was in a position to influence legislation so he could exploit the mineral wealth he now found himself "lording" over.

And exploit it the Dudley family did. People can today visit the ruin of Witley Court in Worcestershire which gives a glimpse of the wealth the Dudley family extracted from the area.

The population of the area expanded dramatically with the development of the mines and furnaces during the 19th century. Workers migrated there from far and wide.

The Birmingham and district (including the Black Country) population stood at just 187,000 in 1801. By 1851 it had grown to 637,000. Ten years later it had expanded to 819,000. The population continued to expand and by 1901 1,289,000 people lived in Birmingham and its districts. In just 100 years the population of the area had grown more than six times over.

The villages in the area grew quickly into towns. The modern day towns of Dudley, Netherton, Old Hill, Cradley Heath, Brierley Hill, Halesowen, Tipton, Coseley, Rowley Regis, Blackheath, Wednesbury, West Bromwich, Oldbury, Smethwick, Sedgley, Bilston and Darlaston all grew during this period to form what is now known as the Black Country.

The expansion of the population in the area is closely matched with the expanding mineral and iron production of the time. Below are figures obtained from T J Raybould's 1973 book, *The Economic Emergence of the Black Country*:

Mineral output of the Black Country

Year	Coal in tons	Ironstone in tons
1800	840,000	60,000
1850	5,000,000	–
1855	7,323,000	–
1859	4,450,000	785,000 [1860]
1865	9,000,000	660,000
1872	9,000,000	642,000

Production of pig iron and the total of blast furnaces in the Black Country

Year	Total furnaces	In blast	Pig iron in tons
1796	14	–	13,210
1806	42	–	49,000
1827	95	–	216,000
1830	123	–	213,000
1840	135	116	364,000 [1839]
1844	135	100	468,000
1852	159	127	743,000 [1854]
1860	181	108	396,000 [1861]
1870	171	114	726,000 [1871]

The tables above give an indication of the rapid growth of both mineral extraction and pig iron production in the area, with the 1860s and 1870s being the height of output for both, correlating strongly with the rapid growth of the population during these years.

By 1860 there were a reported 441 pits, 181 blast furnaces, 118 iron works, 79 rolling mills and 1,500 puddling furnaces within five miles of Dudley. All would have produced the smoke which helped give the area its name.

The sheer quantity of pits and furnaces is characteristic of the specific industrial development of the area. Unlike other industrialising areas that were dominated by a small-ish number of large workplaces, such as the mill towns of the north, the Black Country consisted of many small-scale pits and production points. "Home-working" was also a significant feature of the area, with small-scale furnaces being a feature of many backyards, firstly in the production of nails and then in the production of chain.

The geology of the area may have contributed to this development. The shallowness of the coal seam meant that small-scale extraction from numerous pits was more economical than the need to sink one deep large pit. The iron smelting and pig iron production could be easily located around the numerous pits rather than just one or two large pits.

A low wage industrialisation

G C Allen, in his book *The Industrial Development of Birmingham and the Black Country 1860-1927*, quotes Richard Cobden commenting on the election of John Bright MP in 1857 and pointing out the difference between Manchester and Birmingham:

> I have always had [the opinion] that the social and political state of the town [Birmingham] is far more healthy than that of Manchester: and it arises from the fact that the industry of the hardware district is carried on by small manufacturers...while the great capitalists in Manchester form an aristocracy, individual members of which wield an influence over sometimes 2,000 persons...there is freer intercourse between all classes than in the Lancashire town, where a great and impossible gulf separates the workman from his employer.

Engels also noticed the distinct difference of the area in his work *The Condition of the Working Class in England* back in 1845. After describing the small-scale production in Birmingham and the squalor workers had to suffer he went on to say:

In the iron district of Staffordshire [Black Country] the state of things is still worse. For the coarse wares made here neither much division of labour (with certain exceptions) nor steam power or machinery can be applied. In Wolverhampton, Willenhall, Bilston, Sedgeley, Wednesfield, Darlaston, Dudley, Walsall, Wednesbury, etc, there are, therefore, fewer factories, but chiefly single forges, where the small masters work alone, or with one or more apprentices, who serve them until reaching the twenty-first year... The dwellings are bad and filthy, often so much so that they give rise to disease; and in spite of the not materially unhealthy work, the children are puny, weak, and in many cases severely crippled... In Sedgeley and its surrounding district, where nails form almost the sole product, the nailers live and work in the most wretched stable-like huts, which for filth can scarcely be equalled. Girls and boys work from the tenth or twelfth year, and are accounted fully skilled only when they make a thousand nails a day. For twelve hundred nails the pay is 5 ¾ d. Every nail receives twelve blows, and since the hammer weighs 1 ½ pounds, the nailer must lift 18,000 pounds to earn this miserable pay. With this hard work and insufficient food, the children inevitably develop ill-formed, undersized frames... As to the state of education in this district...it is upon an incredibly low plane; half the children do not go to Sunday school, and the other half go irregularly; very few, in comparison with other districts, can read, and in the matter or writing the case is much worse.

This small-scale labour intensive production was very profitable during the early period of industrialisation and it made huge profits for the Dudley family. However, not concentrating production into larger units had a serious negative impact upon the workers in the area. As G C Allen described:

The nailers found it difficult to improve their position by combining together, while the fact that many branches of their trade were competitive with Birmingham and Wolverhampton cut nail factories intensified the chronic depression of their wages.

So as factories and mechanisation improved efficiencies and profits elsewhere, competitive profits could only be maintained by small-scale producers by cutting wages. Factories and larger workplaces collectivised workers and therefore made combining workers into unions easier. The benefits of collective bargaining over time would help push up wages. Increased mechanisation and larger factories also concentrated the profits for the bosses. Therefore when challenged for higher wages they could usually afford to make some concessions to the workers' demands.

In contrast, smaller-scale production atomised and isolated the workers, making the organising of trade unions more difficult. And it also created the condition where middlemen commissioning out the work could pitch one worker against another. This created a constant downward pressure on wages.

So while on average wages in Britain rose during the second half of the 19th century, it appears this was not the experience of workers in the Black Country.

From papers retained by Arthur Willets, now placed in the Dudley Archives Service, there is a newspaper article from 8 November 1891 describing a strike movement from Old Hill to Bromsgrove which supports the generalisation that the real wage rises secured by workers elsewhere had yet to be won in the Black Country. This *Sunday Chronicle* article appears to have been written by a "Special Commissioner" from the Manchester region, concerned about the appallingly low wages across the Black Country. The reporter firstly refers to the normal working wage of 18s a week seeming like a "kings ransom" to the workers on strike and goes on to plead, if not agitate, for the workers to demand more than the 10 percent they were striking for:

> And I hope, furthermore, that by this time the poor down-trodden souls have perceived the absurdity of striking for an advance of only ten percent, upon miserable wages like theirs. 10 percent advance on ten shillings for a man, and five or six shillings for a woman, is not worth going without one meal.

The strike by thousands of nail makers and chain makers, both men and women, took place as the Earl of Dudley took his new bride home. The reporter draws the contrast between the luxurious life of the Dudleys and the plight of the workers in the area. He also goes on to report meetings of thousands of workers hearing agitators from Manchester describe that male chain makers there earn between 25s and 30s a week and women chain makers 18s a week. The Manchester agitators make the case that if such rates can be paid in Manchester, why not in the Black Country? The meetings subsequently resolve to demand a 50 percent pay rise.

The article does not state if the workers won this strike or not but it did go on to describe how the employers in the area used "divide and rule" tactics to drive wages down:

> One employer on a large scale has two "warehouses" separated by several miles of country, and it is regular custom to lock one set of poor devils out for a week on the pretext that the others had accepted lower terms. Then when they come in at the reduction, the second body hear of it in turn, and are forced to give way.

Cradley Heath and the chain industry
During the later half of the 19th century Cradley Heath became the geographical centre of the chain making

industry, with 90 percent of all chain in Britain being made in the Black Country. Big chains were produced for the ships transporting the increasing trade around the world. The anchorage for the *Titanic* was built two miles away from Cradley Heath, in Netherton. Smaller chains were for other industrial needs and for domestic use. But perhaps most disturbingly, chain was used to enslave Africans and some of the early chain production in Cradley Heath was made for this purpose. Even after 1834, when slavery was abolished across the British Empire, chains for slavery were still produced for the cotton plantations in the US.

During this period organisations representing the chain makers moved their headquarters into the area. The Chain Makers' and Strikers' Association, founded by Thomas Sitch, moved their head office into "Unity Villa" in Cradley Heath in 1899.

The 1911 census figures revealed the concentration of the chain making trade in the area. Out of a total of 7,323 chain makers across England and Wales 6,550 lived in Staffordshire and Worcestershire. The ward of Cradley Heath alone accounted for 2,000 of these.

The Home Office List of 1911 revealed that there were 938 chain workshops (small chain shops as opposed to the chain works making the larger chains) of which 918 were in the Cradley Heath area. Again these figures support the fact that small-scale production remained the dominant feature across the Black Country. The continuing existence of "backyard" workshops meant that both methods of production, and the conditions that workers endured, had not changed since the 18th century.

But while the methods of production had not changed, the demographics of those who did the home-working had. Census figures show that 19.7 percent of all chain makers in 1861 were women. By 1911 this had risen to 32.1 percent.

According to Ron Moss in his book *Chain and Anchor Making in the Black Country*:

In 1910 around 3,500 workers made chain in small work-shops, at home, probably twice as many as the number of workers making chain inside the factories. What was more, around two-thirds of the home workers were women. Many of them had once been employed making nails and had been displaced from that trade by the machine made nails that were being produced in Birmingham from around 1820 onwards. They had found use for their skills of working iron in the fire of their hearths at home. The skilled men made larger chain in the factories.

Not only did the women need to work to supplement the relatively low wages of their men, but children also worked. This was an era before maternity rights, and when childcare was a luxury to be afforded only by the middle classes and above. Outside of any school provision children had to accompany their mothers to work. Many old photographs from the era show children sitting in the corner of the workshop. Once old enough, children helped in the production of the chain.

Ron Moss refers to a report of 1841 investigating child labour in the area:

In the same report is mention of the youngest chain maker that I have seen recorded. The inspector met him while pass-ing through Cradley Wood as he was on his way to see Thomas Holloway at the Saltwells. As they walked along the lad, Thomas Barnsley aged 8 ½ years, talked freely to him. The boy explained that he had worked at chain-making since he was four years old. He said that "I dolly and blow"; this meant that he blew the bellows to keep the fire in the hearth going and then he would hammer on the "dolly", the pivoted

tool which was used to finish off the chain-link… His pay was
3s 6d a week and sometimes 4s a week.

Although legislation passed during the later half of the
19th century restricted the hours children could work, the
harsh reality was that children too young to go to school,
or outside of school hours, would have to spend a large
amount of time in the chain shops with their mothers. The
children either kept out of danger by staying in the corner
of the shop, or helped out in making the chain. Given the
extensive working hours of the women chain makers,
together with the appallingly low wages, there was simply
no alternative.

The existence of children at work was described by the
founder of the National Federation of Women Workers,
Mary Macarthur, on her first visit to Cradley Heath in
1907. After the visit Mary wrote an article entitled "Slaves
of the Forge" in which she described the working conditions she saw:

> they remain level with the anvil in which the chain is beaten,
> or below it on the floor where likely as not a baby, in kicks
> and screams, makes the protest against the narrowness of the
> wooden box in which he is cradled, or against the sparks or
> specks from the forge which light on his face or arms. The
> thoughts of the poor people are with varieties of plain and
> twisted links, with swivels, and hooks, and with the fluctua-
> tions of that daily bread that they win with so much travail.

With improvements in wages and working conditions
being made elsewhere during the latter half of the 19th
century, the plight of workers in Cradley Heath and the
wider area shocked many commentators. One German
researcher described Cradley Heath as "Hell".

In Mary Macarthur's words:

The fame of the district has spread far and wide, and no social investigator from distant lands considers his tour of our country complete without a visit to Cradley Heath...

My first glimpse of Cradley Heath was a dark November afternoon. The train stopped just outside the station and from the window of the carriage I looked down on a long low shed. The iron gratings which served as windows, the red glow of the forge fires and the dim shadows of the toiling workers made me think of some torture chamber from the middle ages.

3.

THE WOMEN CHAIN MAKERS' STRIKE OF 1910

The workers face their situation in different ways. Some succumb to it, allowing themselves to be demoralised: but the increase in drunkenness, vice, crime and irrational spending, is a social phenomenon, the creation of capitalism, and not to be explained by the weakness and shiftlessness of individuals. Others submit passively to their fate and exist as best they can as respectable law-abiding citizens, take no interest in public affairs and thus actually help the middle class to tighten the chains which bind the workers. But real humanity and dignity are to be found only in the fight against the bourgeoise, in the labour movement which the workers' conditions inevitably produce.

—Fredrick Engels, *The Condition of the Working Class in England*, 1845

THE IMPROVEMENTS in wages and conditions gained by many workers during the previous 50 years had passed the chain makers of Cradley Heath by. Women were increasingly the "home-workers" grafting in the back-yard workshops, for extensive hours on extremely low wages, supplementing the low wages of the men. It was only the combination of the men's and women's low wages that made a liveable income and kept hunger at bay.

The average male wage at the time was 27s a week, or £70 a year. Before the 1910 strike women chain makers in Cradley Heath were earning just 5s to 6s for working a 54-hour week—one fifth of the average male wage.

To understand just how low this level of pay was it is worth making a modern day comparison.

According to *Labour Research*, the average full-time male wage in April 2009 was £633 per week, equivalent to £32,916 per annum. One fifth of this wage would be £6,583 per annum, or £126.60 per week.

On a 40-hour week this equates to just £3 an hour. On a 54-hour week, which is what the women chain makers were working, this equates to an hourly rate of £2.35.

The adult minimum wage in 2009 was £5.73 an hour. On a 40-hour week this results in weekly earnings of £229 and annual earnings of £11,918. On a 54-hour week the weekly wage would be £309.

On any measure a 5s or 6s weekly wage was extremely low. By modern British standards it is less than half the current minimum wage.

Why were wages so low?

The extremely low wages paid to mainly (but not exclusively) women domestic chain makers existed because they were unorganised and isolated. They were also pitched competitively against one another to secure work.

This situation was deliberately fostered by the employers in the area. Although in the factories producing the larger chains the employers recognised trade unions and paid better rates, there was a practice of commissioning out production of smaller chains through middlemen. These middlemen then commissioned the work out to individual chain makers in their backyards.

The middlemen creamed off their own "profit" from the gap between the market price of chain and the amount they paid the domestic chain makers. Each domestic chain maker had to individually negotiate a price with the middleman to secure the work and felt they were in no position to negotiate much on top of the miserable rates on offer for fear of losing out to others.

The result of this arrangement was that the larger chain manufacturers and the middlemen both maintained their profits while perpetuating the miserable conditions in Cradley Heath.

It was only possible to live on these miserable wages in a household where they supplemented a man's wages. The lowest rent for a two roomed house with a backyard workshop was 3s a week. On top of this coal and tools were needed. And this was before any food was purchased. Mary Macarthur was called as a witness to give evidence to the House of Commons Select Committee on home-working and the "sweated" trades in 1906. When commenting on the condition of women chain makers in Cradley Heath she contrasted them to the men working in larger, unionised workplaces: "Forty years ago all chain makers were sweated. The men were sweated as well as the women."

Macarthur then went on to explain that the unionisation of the larger workplaces, led by Tom Sitch, had increased the wages of the men but not the largely female home-workers.

Tom Sitch's members received good wages—some of them 15s... Husband and wife working together might count upon £1. Sometimes to help to add to these meagre sums, the children of the family were brought in. Hundreds of infants at Cradley Heath could and did manufacture presentable chain.

While the existence of sweating was denied by hard-nosed employers and Conservatives, its horrendous reality created a campaign to end it once and for all.

Sweating and the wage boards
In 1906 a national exhibition was held in London to draw attention to the existence of "sweating" in Britain.

Its aim was to shock public opinion in the hope that enough pressure would be created to establish legislation outlawing such low levels of pay. One result of the conference was the creation of the Anti-Sweating League.

The Liberal government, in office from 1906, established a select committee to examine the evidence around sweating. Three years later legislation was finally presented to parliament. The Trades Board Act of 1909 laid down minimum wages for four trades in which wages were particularly low, including tailoring, paper box making, machine-made lace and the domestic chain trade. The idea was to establish trades boards for the four industries, which would be made up of employers, employee representatives and a smaller number of appointees, whose job it would be to establish new minimum wage rates.

For years the Chain Manufacturers Association (CMA) had done nothing to tackle the plight of low paid workers. Local employers and Conservatives denied the social problems caused by sweating existed at all, or claimed they were exaggerated. When evidence became undeniable they blamed the poor conditions on the workers themselves. They cited intemperance (drunkenness) as the cause of the terrible social conditions in Cradley Heath. Thus the employers turned reality on its head. Rather than seeing drunkenness as a way of dealing with the dreadful social conditions, it caused it!

The bosses let themselves off the hook, living comfortable waited-upon lives in leafy Stourbridge, yet where the workers lived and worked in Cradley Heath there were no public facilities. There was no free library, no swimming baths and no recreation place for the whole of the area. The only public facilities that did exist were the workhouse and the mortuary.

The employers' sudden conversion was, in part, the result of pressure from the Anti-Sweating League and trade unions, but the final push came with the passing of the act on 1 January 1910.

Previously the chain bosses had boycotted meetings asked for by Tom Sitch's Chain Makers' and Strikers' Union. Suddenly the bosses in the CMA pronounced their support for the trade boards and even tried to claim credit for their trade being included in the legislation.

On 7 January the first meeting of the Chain Trades Board took place. The employers put forward their six representatives, five of whom belonged to the CMA and one represented the 140 or so middlemen. The workers' representatives were Thomas Sitch, William Bate, William Cooper, Josiah Griffiths, Charles Homer and Mary Macarthur.

Five meetings of the Chain Trades Board took place between January and March but there was no settlement in sight. Despite their proclaimed support of the minimum wage the employers were now concerned about the cost. Mary Macarthur was reported to be extremely frustrated at the employers' lack of interest in ending the practice of sweating. Even the more moderate Thomas Sitch, a life-long advocate of conciliation and arbitration between the union and bosses, spoke of his disappointment:

> After six months experience on the board I have come to the conclusion, very reluctantly, that we were living in a fools paradise when we entertained the thought that our employers were anxious to see the trade free from the evils of sweating.

Only following pressure from the three appointed members of the board did the employers finally concede to a minimum wage rate of 11s 3d for a 54-hour week, or 2½d per hour. While this concession was still well below the male average of 27s a week, and somewhat behind the 15s a week earned by male chain makers in the factories, a new rate of 11s 3d nevertheless represented a 100 percent pay rise for the domestic chain makers.

The new rate was announced in May 1910, to come into effect three months later. The act contained a provision for workers to individually contract out of the new rates for a further six months, and the reluctant employers used this loophole to maximum effect.

Many of the middlemen, and some of the smaller employers outside the CMA, went round the chain makers asking them to sign papers opting out of the new minimum rate. Some 1,000 chain makers signed such forms. Many were unable to read or write and so wouldn't have known exactly what they were signing. When it was later pointed out to them what they had done many felt angry for being duped.

At the same time the employers were commissioning more and more work in order to create a stockpile of chain. The employers were planning to destroy the new minimum rate. They would stockpile chain now until the introduction of the increased wage, then reduce orders, thereby creating an artificial slump in demand and increasing unemployment, which they could then blame on the introduction of the new minimum wage rates. The employers' hope was that this would convince the chain workers that the new minimum wage rates were a problem that needed to be scrapped so that everyone could be in work.

In fact, by the time the new rate was due to come into effect on 17 August 1910, the employers had managed to get so many of the chain makers to opt out that they refused to apply it to anyone. They expected little resistance from the unorganised female domestic chain makers.

Faced with such unreasonable employers Mary Macarthur realised that there was only one option left to try and get the new minimum rates enforced. Workers not offered 11s 3d had to go on strike until the new rate was forthcoming.

On 23 August the National Federation of Women Workers, led by Mary Macarthur, to which some 400 women chain makers in Cradley Heath belonged, drafted an agreement stipulating the women's desire to be paid the new minimum wage immediately.

The response from the employers, particularly the 30 or so small factories in the area, was to lock them out.

Mary Macarthur organised a mass meeting for all the domestic chain makers in the area, whether working in a small factory or in their own backyard. The mass meeting attracted a significant crowd of maybe 1,000 women and children.

In her biography of Mary Macarthur M A Hamilton describes how the women at the meeting openly declared their full commitment to the strike:

> One gaunt old woman, raising her hand aloft, declared that she should drop dead rather than sign a contracting-out paper; the others pledged themselves to the same determination. Those who had been misled into signing repudiated their marks or signatures. All were ready to come out and stay out.

The strike had begun.

Solidarity for victory
If the employers thought the women chain makers would be too desperate for money to strike for any length of time, Mary Macarthur was also aware of the imminent hunger and hardship the strikers faced.

She therefore left the immediate organisation of the strike in the capable hands of Julia Varley (who had already recruited many of the women chain makers to the National Federation of Women Workers) and C H Sitch so that she could return to London and begin to raise much needed funds.

Macarthur threw all her energy into this task. Although just 30 years old she had a wealth of experience which set her in good stead for her task. From the trade unionists and socialists in Scotland, where she was from, to her contacts in London, where she now lived and worked, the urgent call for funds would have been made. Macarthur was a member of the Independent Labour Party with its numerous branches around the country, and her involvement in the cross-party Anti-Sweating League put her in touch with some middle class and Conservative sympathisers. Her work for the Women's Trade Union League also meant she would have had some parliamentary contacts.

Armed with this experience and contact base she set about writing leaflets and letters, giving interviews and addressing meetings, all with a view to raising solidarity and support for the strike. Mary also used the power of the cinema, which was in its infancy at the time, to expose the miserable conditions the women chain makers of Cradley Heath had to endure, thereby generating enormous sympathy and solidarity from cinema audiences. The manager of Pathé estimated that this film was seen by around 10 million people throughout the country.

The trade unions responded with financial support, among them the railwaymen, the grocers' assistants, the power loom weavers, the upholsterers, the miners and the engineers.

Macarthur managed to raise support from unlikely quarters: George Cadbury (the chocolate factory owner in Birmingham) gave £5 a week for as long as the strike lasted; a Lady Beauchamp donated £200 (a sum that could pay 800 strikers 5s each for a week); Neville Chamberlain gave £50 and the Countess of Warwick donated £25.

In addition the whole of the Conservative press in the West Midlands supported the strike with one local paper noting:

> From the commencement of the dispute, the women had the advantage of whole hearted sympathy from every class… The knowledge that many of them worked under the most depressing conditions for a mere pittance of 5s and 6s a week touched deeply the human interest of the country. There is no doubt that the women's campaign was handled with consummate skill, and the appeal on behalf of the women chain makers…was irresistible.

Mary Macarthur clearly had an eye for getting the message across in the press. She gathered a dozen of the oldest women chain makers together for photographs and interviews. The oldest chain maker was 79 years old. In these photos the women held placards, asking for funds, with headlines such as "England's Disgrace. Help the women chain makers who are fighting for 2½d an hour". Another placard read "The White Slaves of England".

The strike also gained support among leading churchmen, with the Bishop and Dean of Worcester donating money to the strike fund.

But the dispute did not just gain support within England: it also began to attract notoriety across the world. When Will Anderson, chairman of the Independent Labour Party, attended an international conference in Copenhagen he found the women chain makers' strike at the centre of discussion.

So successful were Mary Macarthur's attempts to raise support that money poured into the strike fund. On 27 August over 300 members of the NFWW on strike received their first week's strike pay of 5s.

In the meantime Julia Varley and C H Sitch ensured

that the strikers remained organised. The strike stayed solid and gained momentum. By 1 September an estimated 650 workers were on strike (more than the total membership in the NFWW), holding daily processions with banners and bands, collecting money as they went along. The joy of the strike was clearly still with them as they marched each day singing songs, including the specially written chain makers' "Marseillaise".

Cradley Heath made around 90 percent of all the chain in Britain. The solid strike by 650 women workers was clearly going to eventually have an impact upon the sales of chain, once the stockpiles were exhausted. There was nowhere else for the employers to get the chain made.

The money being raised meant it was possible to pay the striking women 5s a week to remain on strike. This firstly meant they avoided hunger. But perhaps more importantly, rather than working 54 hours to earn 5s, they spent their days walking the streets, talking to reporters, being in control of their actions. The emancipating feeling must have been exhilarating for those actively involved in the strike.

As the newspaper the *County Advertiser for Staffordshire and Worcestershire* put it:

> The women's blood is up, and they mean to have their emancipation day now…they made a fresh vow to have the eleven shillings and three pence which the Trade Board has laid down as the minimum for a week's work, or to throw down their hammers. It is inconceivable that the employers can hold out against the demand… The chain workers are at last learning the secret of united action.

The Employers feel the pressure
After just a few days of the strike and sensing the general mood the attitude of the larger employers in the Chain

Manufacturers Association (CMA) changed considerably. They realised that they were faced with a potentially lengthy dispute which they could no longer be certain about winning.

The sight of the daily marches, Mary Macarthur's brilliant propaganda, the press response, and the solidarity donations flooding in clearly rocked the employers' early confidence.

Just ten days into the strike the major employers in the CMA agreed to meet the workers' representatives under the auspices of the Chain Trade Board.

The solid nature of the strike and the support it was receiving created divisions among the employers. The large employers in the CMA were dignitaries who attended local churches and chapels. The label of "sweater" was something to avoid. The film being shown in cinemas across the country meant that they could no longer argue that the social conditions in Cradley Heath had been exaggerated.

So they blamed the smaller employers, not part of their organisation, and the middlemen for creating the poverty pay of the domestic chain makers. At the meeting on 2 September the CMA agreed to pay the new minimum rates but claimed that they could not force the smaller employers or middlemen to do the same. In an unexpected twist the large employers in the CMA sought to preserve their profits and strengthen their grip on the trade by cutting out the middlemen. They agreed to pay the new minimum rate of 11s 3d a week on condition that the NFWW guaranteed to financially support all the women strikers who continued to refuse to work for anything less.

While it was never the motivation of Mary Macarthur or the NFWW to help one employer against the other the women strikers had little choice but to go along with the wishes of the CMA, since ending the strike at this point would have meant the smaller employers and middlemen would have won and the minimum wage would have been lost.

However, with all the publicity, funds for the strike continued to roll in. By the second week of the strike donations had been received from over 200 union bodies. Collections were being made outside churches, chapels, factories, trade union meetings and football grounds. There was enough money being raised to pay every striker 5s a week.

The strikers' processions continued and regular mass meetings were held in a local school. On 3 September the number on strike increased to 800 after a procession to Old Hill, one mile away, persuaded more chain makers to join the strike.

The employers in the CMA created what was called a "White List" of employers who agreed to pay the new minimum wage. At first the chain masters outside the CMA refused to sign the White List. So too did the middlemen.

The strike remained solid and fought for more solidarity. In the middle of September a delegation of women chain makers attended the Trades Union Congress in Sheffield. When addressing the conference they held up their chains and explained what little pay they received for making it. The TUC pledged the moral and financial support of the whole trade union movement.

The threat of boycotts was now also in the pipeline. The government announced that they would refuse to tender any contracts to employers not complying with the Trades Board Act. One of the largest private sector chain buyers adopted a similar policy.

As the weeks passed the strike remained solid. The donations flooding in remained above the £200 needed each week to pay the 800 strikers 5s. This meant all the pressure was placed on those employers and middlemen who refused to sign the White List and pay the 11s 3d minimum wage.

The middlemen in particular must have realised that their livelihoods were at stake. The longer the strike lasted the greater the risk of them losing all future business. Slowly but surely the middlemen began to sign the White List and agree the new wage rates. By the time the strike had entered its tenth week the majority of the middlemen had signed up and the employers' association passed a resolution stating that they would only deal with the middlemen who had signed up. (That the CMA did not do this in September shows their reluctance to pay the new rates.)

The middlemen and employers who refused to sign up to the minimum wage were defeated.

The women chain makers' strike was victorious.

On the evening of 22 October 1910, the final day of the strike, the women chain makers once again gathered in the local school in Grainger's Lane.

They sang the chain makers' "Marseillaise" and listened to speeches by trade unionists J J Mallon, C H Sitch, Julia Varley and others. The last speaker was Mary Macarthur. She was met with wild applause. Tears of joy were shed as they heard Macarthur urge everyone to join the union. As the women workers left the school one was reported to have said, "It's too good to be true."

From that day on the women's wages, while still well below the average male wage, were doubled.

The impact of victory

The victory had a dramatic impact upon the lives of the women chain makers. Not only were they financially better off, the victory boosted their confidence enormously. They now understood their collective power. The membership of the NFWW in Cradley Heath grew from 400 before the strike to 1,700.

But the victory also boosted the confidence of workers across the region. Thousands of unskilled and unorganised workers in factories and workshops across the Black Country—men and women—earning as little as 20s (£1) a week, revolted. All won recognised wage rates and trade union organisation grew.

The story of the chain makers' strike had reached 10 million people in cinemas across the country. The news of victory provided a lesson that workers can improve their conditions by taking action. Therefore the victory must have fed into the mood that saw the number of strikes and trade union membership increase dramatically during the period 1910-1914, known as the Great Unrest.

The oldest women chain makers pose for a photograph to raise solidarity and support for the strike.

4.

MARY MACARTHUR

YOU HAVE all heard of the foolish old woman who went out and bought a bundle of sticks tied tightly together with a piece of string. She was in a hurry to get the fire lit when she came home, so she tried to break the bundle as it was. What was the result? She did not break the sticks. She nearly broke her fingers instead. Had she untied the string, each stick could easily have been broken separately, but united together the sticks protected each other and could not be broken.

A trade union is like a bundle of sticks. The workers are bound together and have the strength of unity. No employer can do as he likes with them. They have the power of resistance. They can ask for an advance without fear. A worker who is not in a union is like a single stick. She can easily be broken or bent to the will of her employer. She has no power to resist a reduction in wages. If she is fined, she must pay without complaint. She dare not ask for a "rise". If she does she will be told, "Your place is outside the gate; there are plenty to take your place." An employer can do without one worker. He cannot do without all his workers. If all the workers united in a union—as strong as the bundle of sticks—complain or ask for improved conditions, the employer is bound to listen.

Sometimes a few of the most sensible and wide awake women in a factory decide to join a union. They cannot, however, persuade the more thoughtless and selfish girls to join. They say, "Oh, we don't need to join. We'll get any benefits you get." Such girls are not only selfish, they are short-sighted. They are injuring not only themselves, but their fellow workers as well. They are standing in the way of improved conditions. They are assisting their employer to keep wages down, to make reductions, to inflict fines, or to provide bad material.

The above was written by Mary Macarthur and published in the paper she edited, the *Woman Worker*, in 1907. She goes on to urge workers to get fellow workers to join a union. The "Bundle of Sticks" is an example of how Mary could explain the union cause in a straightforward manner and motivate people at the same time.

Mary's leadership of the Cradley chain makers was not a one-off. An important victory in itself, her leadership during this strike is just one of many significant contributions Mary made to the labour movement in Britain, in particular for working women.

When reading about Mary Macarthur you end up reading compliment after compliment of her organising, agitational, tactical and negotiating skills. Her drive to succeed impresses not only her trade union and socialist comrades of the time, but also those in positions of power, whether employers or the government.

But most importantly, Mary Macarthur quickly gained the admiration of those workers, mainly women, who she so skilfully organised and represented.

In her biographical sketch of Mary Macarthur, M A Hamilton recalls one anecdote from Mary's campaign as the first British female candidate for parliament in 1918. Given the patriotic fervour during the First World War, anti-war candidates received abuse and hostility, and Mary was perceived to be such a candidate by her opponents. While holding a street meeting in the Black Country town of Lye, in the then constituency of Stourbridge, Mary was unsure how a large group of male workers marching up to the meeting would react. But her status among workers in the area was such that they sang to her and greeted her fraternally as "our Mary". And it is on that basis that I will use her first name as reference for this chapter.

The beginnings of a class fighter

Born 1880 in Glasgow and named Mary Reid Macarthur, she was one of three surviving daughters. Mary's father owned a drapery business and the family was relatively well off, with the business employing a number of workers. Mary's father was a prominent individual in Glasgow and was a Conservative in politics, with strong anti trade union and even stronger anti-socialist views. In 1895 the family moved to Ayr and Mary, aged just 15, began bookkeeping for her father's business.

She also began writing for the local press and wanted to become a writer. It was in this role at the age of 20 that she was to have her first experience of the trade union movement. The Shop Assistants' Union was attempting to build a branch in Ayr. Upon hearing of this Mary's father sent her to spy on the meeting. In Mary's own words:

> I went to a meeting at Ayr to write a skit on the proceedings. Going to scoff, I remained to pray. I became impressed with the truth and meaning of the labour movement.

The meeting was addressed by John Turner, who asked Mary to join the union. She reportedly declined but urged all the other women in the meeting to join, which would have undoubtedly annoyed her father. The skit was never written.

Impressed by their first meeting, John Turner kept in contact with Mary and eventually convinced her to join the union. He soon offered her the position of chair for the Ayr branch of the Shop Assistants' Union.

Mary was at first hesitant to make the move towards trade unionism, but she was convinced of the cause.

Accepting the position of chair was to be the first step in a radically changed life.

The Scottish section of the Shop Assistants' Union was in close contact with numerous socialist societies around at that time. John Turner was a revolutionary anarchist and Will Anderson (Mary's future husband) was a socialist in the Independent Labour Party (ILP).

Mary's organising talents shone through and in 1902, at the age of 22, she became the president of the Scottish National District Council of the Shop Assistants' Union. While attending a national conference she met the socialist Margaret Bondfield, who she stayed with on moving to London in 1903. At the age of 23 she became the secretary of the Women's Trade Union League.

The Women's Trade Union League

The Women's Trade Union League had been founded in 1874 to redress the underpayment of women workers. The Board of Trade Enquiry into Earnings and Hours of 1909 reported on wage rates in 1906. While the average male wage was 25s 9d a week, women in the cotton industry (with good union organisation) earned 18s 8d a week. With the average female wage at 10s 10½d a week there were clearly a number of trades in which women earned far less than the average.

It was deemed acceptable by many that women should earn less than men, even for doing the same job. Women were not entitled to vote. Even some of the craft unions still excluded women from being members of their trades, for fear of reducing the wages of men.

The Women's Trade Union League had been established by sympathetic middle class men and women who recognised the value of trade union organisation campaigned within the wider union movement for recognition, but rejected the militant method of strikes to achieve their

BREAKING THEIR CHAINS

aims. Despite this, its strength in the early 1900s was largely due to the affiliation of two powerful unions that recruited both men and women, the Cotton Operatives and the Shop Assistants.

Mary's task as secretary of the league was to organise the most difficult sections of women workers to improve their pay and conditions. She herself summarised the difficulty she faced: "Women are badly paid and badly treated because they are not organised and they are not organised because they are badly paid and badly treated."

Nonetheless, she threw herself into it. According to M A Hamilton:

> Up and down the country she rushed, and everywhere the people with whom she came into contact—the hosiery and boot and shoe workers in the Midlands, the hard pressed folk of the Potteries and the Black Country, the Yorkshire and Lancashire textile operatives, the Dundee jute workers, the Paisley thread girls, the London tailoresses and telephonists—felt her passage like a breathe of hopeful life. This, rather than anything specially original in her organising, was her secret. She gave them hope.

In fact, Mary was so adept at inspiring workers that early on she realised that she needed to adopt a more measured approach. In Mary's own words when addressing the National Women's Trade Union League of America in 1909:

> About the first time I started an open-air meeting I got a number of girls around me on a street corner and I told them about unionism. I was very enthusiastic, and perhaps I gave it to them in too glowing terms. They believed me, and gave me their names to join the union. Ten days afterwards the girls looked more inclined to mob me than anything else,

and I asked them what was the matter. "Oh, we've been ten days in the union and our wages haven't gone up yet!" Of course that taught me it was a mistake. I never speak at a meeting of non-union girls without telling them the union is not an automatic machine.

By 1905, after just two years as secretary, over 60 trade unions had affiliated to the Women's Trade Union League, but more importantly 14,000, new members had also joined. Mary also became the first female member of the London Trades Council.

Political influences

During Mary's first few years in London she explored the many political ideas around at that time. For a brief period she tried being a vegetarian and also tried being teetotal.

Mary's first political influence had been John Turner, who was a revolutionary anarchist. He stressed the importance of industrial action to achieve aims but was "anti-political" when it came to parliament, which he viewed as a waste of time. Will Anderson had also been an early influence. He was an active trade unionist and socialist who was a member of the ILP. Later he was to rise to prominence within the ILP, becoming one of its first MPs.

Margaret Bondfield had left the Marxist Social Democratic Federation (SDF) to join the ILP. At this time the SDF was the largest Marxist organisation in Britain. It advocated revolution to achieve socialism, but did not see the value of industrial action, seeing such demands as wage rises as accepting the premises of capitalism. Despite this many of the early trade union militants of the time owed their political education to the SDF.

Another strong political current was syndicalism, which stressed the sole importance of strikes to advance the conditions of workers, which would result in workers forming syndicates that would become the basis of workers' control of society and thereby establish socialism. Trade unionists such as Tom Mann stood in this tradition.

Mary's early work for the Women's Trade Union League required her to frequent the lobby corridors of parliament. She saw how legislation could be used to improve people's working lives. Therefore the abstentionist position of the anarchists did not fit with her experience. However, she also knew the importance of union organisation and appreciated the power of a strike to force concessions from employers. The SDF's lack of involvement in industrial struggle meant that she was not attracted to them.

The individuals who most inspired and influenced Mary were members of the Independent Labour Party. This included her early friendships with Will Anderson and Margaret Bondfield, and she also greatly admired Keir Hardie. The ILP was a political home where Mary could use her influence to change legislation in parliament while simultaneously recruiting to the trade unions and leading strike action against employers to improve working conditions.

Mary is often referred to as a woman of action rather than theory. While there is no theoretical book by Mary herself she clearly had read and understood the ideas of socialism. This is her presentation to a Parliamentary Select Committee in 1909:

> Forty years ago all the chain makers were sweated. The men were sweated as well as the women. The makers of the great chains that hold ships to their anchorage were sweated; so were the makers of the trivial chains that hold a gate to its post. The man who brought light into this darkness was Tom Sitch, a labour leader of the old school and the founder of the

Amalgamated Society of Anchorsmiths and Shackle Makers. Tom Sitch was not a socialist. He had probably never heard of Karl Marx. He never talked of the class war or understood the theory of "surplus value"...

This suggests Mary *had* read Karl Marx and *did* understand the theory of surplus value. She hated the injustice of low pay and in particular how employers underpaid women workers. Eradicating low pay (sweating) and improving the pay of the poorest workers was where Mary directed much of her early political energy.

The Anti-Sweating League

Mary was centrally involved in the cross-party group which organised the Exhibition of Sweated Industries in 1906. Hundreds of thousands visited the London exhibition over the summer and most visitors were shocked by what they saw.

The outcome of the exhibition was the formation of the Anti-Sweating League, and Mary joined the executive committee.

One of the first tasks she faced was convincing the trade union movement of the necessity of wage boards to enforce a minimum wage. At a three-day conference of over 300 trade union representatives Mary had to use all her tact and persuasive oratory in order to win the conference to the demand. As the conference developed there were an increasing number of delegations making contributions critical of such boards. These reportedly included some members of the SDF, who viewed the wage boards as a means of compromising with capitalism rather than overthrowing it. To avoid the disaster of the conference failing to back the demand for the wage boards, Mary is reported to have made a passionate intervention, reminding delegates of the dire conditions many workers in the sweated industries had to endure day in day out, and the urgent need to end this injustice. M A Hamilton describes Mary's intervention as one that united the whole conference into supporting the resolution for the wage boards, "carried by acclamation amid resounding cheers".

The formation of the National Federation of Women Workers

Mary's early trade union and political campaigning took place at a time when the labour movement was growing, albeit from a small base. But as anyone involved with the labour movement will know, not every initiative ends in success. Indeed it was a defeat that Mary experienced that convinced her of the need to establish a new national trade union for women, the National Federation of Women Workers (NFWW).

The Women's Trade Union League was not set up in a way that would allow it to affiliate to the General Federation of Trade Unions and thereby give access to strike pay for its members. Each group would set up its own branch accounts and then affiliate to the league, so if any group took strike action they had to secure funds themselves.

Aware of this, the jute workers of Dundee requested a 5 percent pay rise, but stated that they would not go on strike. Seeing the weakness of the workers the employers simply locked them out. Despite Mary spending a week agitating in Dundee the dispute ended in defeat. To avoid this happening again Mary sought to secure an organisation that could pull on national resources for strike pay. She established the National Federation of Women Workers (NFWW) with 2,000 members and 17 branches, affiliated to the trade union movement. Conflict with the Women's Trade Union League was avoided as Mary was both president of the NFWW and secretary of the league.

From editor to agitator

In 1907 Mary returned from an American conference with new ideas on how to organise. She established a penny paper called the *Woman Worker*. At first it was published monthly but soon became a weekly with a circulation of 20,000. The paper was partly written by Mary herself, and she gave space to the debates that were taking place within the trade union movement. These included the suffragettes, the campaign against sweating and news of industrial and political struggles, such as the miners' demand for an EIGHT-hour working day. Although proud enough to sell her own paper on the streets, Mary found the role of editor restrictive and in 1908 gave it up, saying, "One cannot be agitator and editor at the same time, and I—well, it is not that I choose to be, but I am agitator first."

The Great Unrest, 1910-1914

The chain makers' strike in Cradley Heath took place at the very start of a period in British history often called the "Great Unrest". In 1902 2 percent of all workers took industrial action. In 1911 it was over 9 percent. And while not all strikes would end in victory, it was a period when most strikes resulted in the employers having made concessions or backed down. Total trade union membership in Britain rose from 2½ million in 1910 to 4 million by 1914.

After the victory of the Cradley chain makers, boiler-makers and ship builders were in dispute. In October 1910 cotton operatives went on strike, followed in November by miners from South Wales. Mary threw her energies into this period and it was perhaps the Bermondsey strikes in London where she made her biggest impression.

The rising level of industrial action was a sign of the anger and frustration at the rich increasing their profits and wealth while rising prices were reducing real wages. One morning in August 1911 a group of women workers in a large confectionery factory had had enough, left work and marched through the squalid industrial area of south London. As they marched past factories they attracted other workers to come out on strike with them. In total 20 separate strikes joined together as one. Mary threw herself into supporting these strikes immediately. She began to hold meetings with the strikers from 6am each morning.

There were 20 separate employers who all had to be negotiated with to secure the improvements in pay and conditions that the strikers demanded. However, there was also the immediate need to feed the women and children on strike. On the first day of the Bermondsey strikes Mary wrote a letter to the press appealing for money:

> Many thousands of women are on strike, many more are locked out, the pawnshops are closed and outdoor relief refused. As wages for many women in the jam, pickle, glue and tin box trades range from 7s to 9s weekly when at work there is no margin for a crisis of this kind.
>
> The plight of the children is pitiable. We want at least a thousand loaves of bread at the Labour Institute, Fort Road, Bermondsey, SE, if possible by noon on Monday. Who will send them?

Within a week £500 had been raised.
The *Daily Chronicle*, 15 August 1911, reported:

> The women seemed to be in the highest spirits. They went laughing and singing through Bermondsey, shouting, "Are we downhearted?" and answering the question by a shrill chorus of "No!" It was noticeable that many of them had put on their "Sunday Best". In spite of the great heat, hundreds of them wore fur boas and tippets—the sign of self-respect.

A great meeting of 15,000 men, women and children—all on strike—assembled in Southwark Park. It was addressed by Mr Ben Tillett and other Labour leaders. But the leader of this army of revolt is Miss Macarthur, of the Women's Federation.

Thousands of loaves were distributed daily from Bermondsey Institute and the NFWW recruited 4,000 members.

After three weeks of strike action wage rises had been gained from 18 of the 20 employers that Mary and the NFWW were in charge of. The increases ranged from 1s to 4s a week. The greatest gain was in raising the spirits and hopes of some of the most downtrodden workers in London.

Mary and the National Federation of Women Workers were involved with strike after strike during this period. In 1912 Mary led the Bridport net workers, the Kidderminster carpet girls and many others.

The Great War, 1914-1918

The heady times of the Great Unrest were also the time when Mary suffered the personal tragedy of having her first baby stillborn in 1913. M A Hamilton suggests this may in part have been due to stress and overwork. At the same time the world was heading towards the enormous tragedy of the First World War.

Before war broke out both Mary and her husband Will Anderson had campaigned against it. Mary urged all NFWW members to attend peace rallies. However, the anti-war sentiment was not the dominant view within the Labour Party and the trade union movement. As soon as war was declared most Labour leaders and trade union leaders got swept away with the patriotic fervour that gripped the country. Instead of opposing the senseless slaughter of this imperialist war, they backed it and suspended strike action.

Mary was momentarily stunned by the sudden impact of patriotism. She was "an internationalist by conviction and a hater of violence by instinct". However, unlike her husband, Mary stopped being publicly critical of the war. Being a woman of action, and less so of theory, probably made it more difficult for Mary to politically deal with the impact of war fever. Mary was keen to ensure that the gains achieved during the Great Unrest were not lost and therefore chose to join government bodies to continue the pursuit of better pay and conditions for women, rather than maintain a principled public opposition to war.

As the war went on more women were needed in the factories, both to directly replace the men volunteering and to meet the increased demand for armament production.

Mary set to the task of organising the women workers in order to prevent employers getting women to do the men's jobs on women's wage rates. It was in this period that the demand "equal pay for equal work" was first raised.

Mary's strategy was first to organise and recruit the new women workers to the union, and second to press for legislation to secure existing wages and conditions.

The need to recruit women workers was also recognised by the male dominated unions, which had previously not supported the demand for a minimum wage for women. The wartime situation now meant the engineers sought an alliance with the NFWW and subsequently adopted the demand for a minimum wage. The war situation also pressurised prime minister Lloyd George to promise to "abolish sweating on war work".

However, the legislation passed in the first Munitions Act of July 1915 did nothing to eradicate sweating. In fact, the legislation increased the powers of the employers to exploit workers since it made strikes illegal and also made it illegal for workers to leave their jobs for better pay or conditions.

This enraged Mary and her response was, "If you say to women you are not to leave employment then you must make the conditions of employment decent."

The opposite happened. The employers exploited the new army of women workers. Most were working between 70 and 80 hours a week for between 9s and 15s. No doubt the employers used patriotism to justify such low pay for such long hours.

The government eventually conceded establishing a Labour Supply Committee to examine the working conditions developing as the war went on. Once again Mary saw an opportunity to use a combination of legislation and industrial muscle to improve the pay and conditions of women workers. She joined the committee and used the position to issue circulars telling employers what they must do. One such circular made it clear that the minimum rate of pay for women should be 20s and women's piece-work rates should be the same as men's. Another stressed the importance of employers providing lavatory and cloakroom facilities. The Ministry of Munitions adopted these circulars but many employers refused to enact them.

When one group of shell makers from Glasgow, who belonged to the NFWW, were refused the conditions of the circulars Mary seized her chance to organise the workers into demanding their implementation. The NFWW organised workers' meetings and, despite it being illegal, gave the employers one week to pay 20s a week or face a strike.

Fearing such a strike could spark off industrial action across the whole of Glasgow, which at that time had the most militant trade union stewards in the country, the employers backed down immediately and paid the 20s a week.

Although prices rose sharply during the war, in particular the price of food which increased by 85 percent during 1917, women's wages increased at a greater rate. At the start of the war in 1914 there were 358,000 women in trade unions. By the end of the war in 1918 this had increased to 1,960,000. Women had on average seen their real wages increase by 50 percent.

Towards the end of the war a number of disputes over equal pay arose. A report in the *Daily Express*, 11 September 1918, entitled "Equal Pay in Lifts?— Ministers May Have to Walk Upstairs" is perhaps the most appealing to recall:

> Cabinet and other ministers, permanent officials, and their armies of clerks in six-storeyed government offices are faced with the prospect of having to climb the stairs instead of being whisked to their rooms by lift. The lift girls are in revolt.
>
> Their story, as related by Miss Mary Macarthur, secretary of the National Federation of Women Workers, to which they belong, has its serio-comic side as an example of how not to deal with grievances.
>
> "These girls are doing work formerly done by men," said Miss Macarthur to a *Daily Express* representative last night. "Men, where they are still employed, receive 8d an hour, plus £1 a week, plus 12½ percent additional bonus, making a total of 59s a week. The girls are paid 5d an hour, plus 5s a week bonus, a total of 25s a week. They felt the injustice of the disparity, and on July 22 we wrote on their behalf to the Office of Works asking for more equal treatment."

After rejecting an initial increase of 4s a week, Mary Macarthur states at the end of the newspaper article, "I shall be surprised if next week members of the Cabinet do not have to walk upstairs to their rooms."

Women and the vote

The injustice of denying half the population the vote because they happened not to be born male inevitably created the conditions in which women would campaign for the vote. The Suffragettes ran a long campaign for female suffrage, but the movement was largely middle class in its composition. For years many male MPs had resisted any extension of the franchise to women on the most reactionary grounds. But as pressure mounted the manoeuvrings and political debates centred around a partial extension of the franchise to middle class women only.

Before the war this caused debates and splits within those forces that wanted to see women get the vote. Early on Mary Macarthur was against a proposed extension of the franchise to propertied women, which would deny working class women the vote. Mary's view was based purely on class lines because she felt that any partial extension would merely extend the period before working class women would get the vote. In addition she believed that organising women into unions would bring more improvements into their lives than the extension of the voting franchise and seems to have viewed the Suffragette campaign as a distraction from this task.

Other forces within the labour movement failed to back the limited extension of the vote because they were still influenced by the sexist attitudes of the time. After years of political manoeuvres and the absence of any progress on the issue Mary argued a different line at the 1912 Labour Party conference.

The Liberal government was now proposing legislation to extend the right to vote, but only to working class men. Under these proposals no women were to be given the right to vote.

At the conference Mary argued that Labour should finally take a stand unambiguously on the women's side and refuse to support any extension to the franchise unless it included women. She passionately argued that if Labour backed the Liberal bill it would simply line itself up with all those misogynists who wanted to continue denying women the vote. Mary won the debate and vote.

Despite all the procrastination and debates before the war, all women above the age of 30 were granted the vote in 1918. What was previously incomprehensible now occurred without any opposition. While women had to wait until 1928 to have the same right to vote as men, it was an important step forward. After all, given the huge contribution women had made to the war effort those who viewed women as "unfit" to vote found it difficult to continue with such idiotic arguments.

For peace and socialism

War on Germany's eastern front had ended in 1917 when workers, led by the Bolsheviks, successfully executed a socialist revolution and established a workers' state for the very first time in history.

War in the west ended on 11 November 1918 after German soldiers refused to fight in the trenches any longer and instead turned their guns on the generals and the Kaiser, who had sent so many to their slaughter. The revolt by German soldiers forced Germany to surrender. This was greeted as a victory by the Allies. Given the huge human cost of the war, armistice was no doubt greeted with a huge sense of relief and jubilation.

Seeking to exploit this mood, a snap general election was announced for December, before many of the soldiers had even returned from France. The extension of the vote to all working class men and all women over 30 meant this election would see the highest ever number of workers participate, boosting hopes that Labour would win a significant number of seats.

Mary accepted the nomination to be the Labour Party's candidate for the constituency of Stourbridge, becoming the first female parliamentary candidate in Britain.

The election was held in an atmosphere that saw anti-war candidates receive huge levels of criticism and smears. Although Mary had been publicly silent on her anti-war sentiments during the war, her election address ran against the popular mood by arguing for a peace. Point 1 of her address (reprinted on pages 82-87) read as follows:

1. A people's permanent peace
There must be NO MORE WAR...The Peace settlement must be based on Justice and Equity between the nations.

This was very much against the mood of the time which was more "hang the Kaiser" than "let's make peace".

There were two other candidates contesting the Stourbridge constituency. One was a pro-war Liberal, Mr Wilson, and the other a pro-war Mr Fisher of the National Democratic Party. Mr Fisher heavily criticised and smeared Mary by calling her a pacifist, defeatist and Bolshevik.

But this was not the only barrier Mary faced. Throughout her political and trade union activity, including during the chain makers' strike, she was known as Mary Macarthur. Despite this the Returning Officer would not allow Mary to use this name on the voting papers. Instead she was forced to use her less familiar married name of Mary Anderson.

When the results were announced all the anti-war candidates did badly. Will Anderson lost his "safe seat" in Sheffield. Ramsay MacDonald lost in Leicester. Liberals who were against the war also did badly.

The pro-war Liberal won the Stourbridge seat with 8,940 votes compared to Mary's 7,587. Obviously disappointed, Mary greeted the result with the comment, "Better be right than top."

On top of this political disappointment quickly followed personal tragedy, when her husband suddenly died in February 1919 from the flu epidemic that swept the country.

After the horrors of the First World War Mary saw her number one political priority being to ensure that there was a lasting peace so that the death and destruction would not be repeated.

Mary was no Bolshevik. She did not seek to emulate the workers' revolution in Russia. Before the war she had been a brilliant class fighter who had thrown all her political energy into winning industrial disputes to advance the cause of the working class. However, when the industrial struggles developed in Britain during 1919-1920, Mary, like many other Labour Party leaders, was absent from the struggle. Instead they saw social change coming through the election of Labour MPs to parliament. The extension of the vote to the working class meant the number one priority of the Labour Party was to get elected. The class struggle was of secondary importance. In practice class struggle was now largely seen as either unimportant or even a barrier to the main aim of building support for the next election.

In January 1919 the Clyde Workers Committee called for a 40-hour week with no loss of pay. Sixty thousand workers went on strike in Glasgow and a general strike developed throughout the whole of Scotland in February. For a moment the red flag was raised in Glasgow. But without the movement spreading to England, the troops and the tanks that were sent to Glasgow wrested control from the militant workers. A total of 35 million days of strike action were taken in 1919—and at one point even the police were on strike in London and Liverpool. This period saw Britain on the brink of revolution.

But unlike Russia, there was not a significant revolutionary socialist party across Britain that could link and coordinate the struggles and shape the revolutionary mood that fermented during 1919. Left wing trade union leaders compromised with Lloyd George, effectively selling the strikes out and sending workers back to work with minor reforms.

Just a few months later Mary herself was to become seriously ill with cancer and doctors did not give her long to live. However, there was enough time for her to make arrangements for the organisational bodies that she had led so brilliantly. She never desired to see a permanent separate organisation for women workers and during her agitation had always stressed the need for men and women workers to unite. She therefore made arrangements for the National Federation of Women Workers to become a section within the National Union of General Workers (which is today known as the GMB) and for the Women's Trade Union League to become a section of the TUC.

After undergoing a second operation in the October of 1920, Mary died on 1 January 1921, aged 40.

Below is what her close friend, Margaret Bondfield, wrote in the introduction to the biographical sketch of Mary Macarthur:

> Mary Macarthur lived a short life; but it was crowded and thrilling. From the moment of contact with the labour movement she forsook repose. Henceforward she lived in storm and stress: in a continuous whirl. She was involved in strikes in which she went on picket duty before daybreak and sometimes rallied her faint hearted followers in meetings continued beyond midnight; she was an editor, so pleased with her paper that she went on the streets to sell it; she was a leader of great processions of work-girls, and with speeches in Trafalgar Square wrung money for them out of disapproving, indifferent or niggardly onlookers. It was a panting, breathless life sustained with unfaltering verve, courage and determination

to achieve. This was one aspect of Mary Macarthur, and had there been no other she would rank high among her contemporaries in the labour movement for the force and ardour of her advocacy; the fixity and fervour, even the fury of her zeal; and for the skill, sometimes attaining to genius, of her leadership. There is, however, another aspect. Potent in action, Mary Macarthur did not lack the complementary qualities of a great captain. In the throes of a strike she seemed in flame, but in preparing and planning her brain was cool and critical. She was masterful in discussion, but also persuasive and subtle and swift. Sometimes, too, she had prevision and could anticipate confidently results and consequences which to our slower minds seemed unlikely or impossible. It is the union in her of these two sets of qualities which renders her distinctive and great. To her other gifts were added common sense and good humour. Often on fire, she was never fanatical, and she would readily come out of passion or excitability to enjoy any fun that might be poked at her. A woman so abundantly endowed could not labour unfruitfully. Nor did she. She has left all working women, the labour movement, and the community as a whole, for ever in her debt.

5.

LESSONS FOR TODAY

THERE ARE some who see the historical struggles undertaken by workers and trade unionists as something firmly set in the past and not relevant for today since materially we live in a richer society. Despite better material conditions in Britain the relationship between employer and employee, boss and worker, is essentially the same one hundred years later. Employers under capitalism still have the incentive to reduce wages in order to maximise profits and workers still have a material interest to increase wages in order to maximise their income. Conflict is built into the social structure of capitalism. When the economy is booming employers can avoid conflict by increasing wages. However, when the economy goes into decline it is workers who are expected to pay the price in wage cuts, social wage cuts (in public services and benefits) or through job cuts, just so the rich can preserve their profits.

Again there is nothing inevitable about the outcome. As Mary Macarthur pointed out in her "Bundle of Sticks" analogy, if the union is strong enough the employer cannot break it.

While the trade union movement in Britain is somewhat bigger than it was in 1910, it would be fair to say that the movement today does not wield the influence and power that it did in the 1970s. The Tories' attempts to smash the trade union movement in the 1980s resulted in a number of defeats for trade unions, most notably the miners' strike of 1984-85. While weakened, the trade union movement is still very much alive. There are still 6 ½ million workers belonging to a trade union. Trade unions still have the potential power to cause significant disruption and pressurise both employers and the government.

The women chain makers' strike shows that the most unorganised and downtrodden workers can discover the secret of united action and change their circumstances for the better. All those workers currently not in trade unions and at the mercy of the whim of their employers have always got the potential power to change their situation. If workers get together, organise and use their industrial muscle, they will see the potential power that they have to make even the most belligerent employers back down and eat humble pie. What may appear to be unobtainable today can become a reality tomorrow.

Trade union leaders, hope and solidarity

Mary Macarthur was, by her own description, an agitator, who had the ability to give the most downtrodden workers the hope that they could improve their lot. She had the ability to inspire workers into action and on many occasions led workers to victory, turning the vision of hope into a reality.

Trade union leaders today would undoubtedly recruit more workers if they could sprinkle a bit of hope in the workplaces that are not fully unionised or in places where no union organisation exists.

After years of union merger upon union merger, today's union bodies tend to be much bigger organisations. When some unions are over a million members it would indeed take some doing for a general secretary to meet every one of their members. Instead there are now layer upon layer of bureaucratic positions supporting a union structure that can sometimes be slow and sluggish to respond when members are angry about issues or events. Indeed some full-time union officials have "careers" to pursue rather than the class struggle. Combined with the anti trade union laws this results in any legal industrial action often taking months to organise, by which time the anger can all too easily be dissipated and the mood for action lost. Not surprisingly, more militant workers sometimes conclude that taking quick unofficial action can bring better and quicker results.

Alongside agitation and inspiration Macarthur also helped to deliver the solidarity required to allow workers to take strike action. Any industrial conflict becomes a battle of strength between employers and workers. If employers can sense workers won't strike for more than a week they can ride the action out. However, if the employers see floods of solidarity money supporting a solid dispute then all the pressure to give in falls upon them. Despite the size of today's modern trade unions how often are members asked to contribute to a particular dispute in one part of the country? The act of raising solidarity is one that needs to be rebuilt so that when a group of workers take action the hope that union power can give is once again turned into reality.

"Sweating" today

The kind of conditions and the levels of pay for workers in Britain today are generally not as bad as those described by Engels in 1845 or those that the women chain makers had to endure. The introduction of the minimum wage in 1999 did at last remove some of the super-exploitation where workers could be legally employed for as little as £1 an hour.

However, such conditions can be seen in the newly industrialising economies around the world. Child labour still occurs in many places. Once a year such conditions appear on our TV screens while people are trying to raise money for Red Nose Day. But no matter how much charity is raised, year after year the same images and stories are replayed. What the chain makers' strike shows is that workers and children suffering such horrible conditions can improve their own circumstances by discovering the key of united action. The international approach to trade unionism is needed more than ever, given the globalised nature of production and trade.

As uncomfortable a thought as it may be, "sweating" does take place in Britain today. The workers who are super-exploited and live in the worst of conditions, like those described by Engels, are migrant workers. Exploitative employers maximise their profits by employing migrant workers on a pittance, below the minimum wage, often deducting money for appalling living conditions, and often in complete disregard of health and safety. This underbelly of Britain sometimes comes to our attention when disasters occur such as the deaths of the migrant cockle pickers in Morecambe Bay. These employers operate outside the law and are rarely brought to justice.

How often are bad employers paraded on the front of newspapers for breaking the law and committing crimes that makes other people's lives a misery?

How often are employers fined for not paying the minimum wage?

To stop this "sweating" in Britain today it seems that exactly the same tactics as those used by Mary Macarthur are needed. There is a real challenge for the trade union movement to actively seek to recruit such workers, and organise them to enforce the legal minimums, thereby improving their pay and conditions.

Women and equal pay today

Despite all the campaigns and legislation there is still a disparity between the pay of men and women today. On the basis of average full-time hourly earnings, excluding over-time, the gender pay gap for full time workers was 17.1 percent in 2008.

While it is largely accepted today that women should be paid the same as men if they do the same job, the difference in pay arises from a form of gender apartheid that views jobs dominated by women as less worthy than those dominated by men. Such job roles would include cleaning, caring roles and retail jobs, all largely (but not exclusively) dominated by female workers. Many such jobs employ workers on, or just above, the minimum wage, sometimes on a temporary basis.

While legislation exists that compels public sector bodies to ensure they employ workers on the basis of "equal pay for equal value" the pressure from business leaders persuaded the Labour government not to extend this to the private sector.

But the real cure for such underpayment is the same as for the women chain makers of Cradley Heath in 1910. Union organisation and industrial action could force employers within such sectors and trades into paying better rates. Those in the "caring" jobs are often black-mailed into thinking about the vulnerable people they care for, chaining them to perpetual low pay. Only by breaking the chains of such blackmail and organising against the employers will their lot be improved.

So too for those in the retail sector, where the casualisation of employment is often used to make workers feel vulnerable. The potential power of such workers is immense, given the immense profits made by such organisations as the major supermarkets.

But to achieve equality on the same basis as men is in reality not equality at all. It is plain to see that not all men are paid the same. The billionaire banker is somewhat better paid than the refuse worker. "Equality" under capitalism means perpetuating the huge class differences that are growing. Getting more women into top positions in society does not by itself improve the conditions for most women.

Mary Macarthur's principled class position on the extension of the voting franchise to women is the kind of position that will ensure all women benefit from "equality", and not just those fortunate enough to climb the corporate ladders.

Trade unions and political representation

Despite Labour governments enjoying huge majorities since they defeated the unpopular Tories in 1997, most of the Tory anti trade union laws have remained in place. Labour has pursued many policies against the interests of the trade unions, particularly in the public sector. It has pushed the logic of the free market and privatisation into parts of the public sector even Margaret Thatcher could not reach. And at times it have gone out of its way to smash or severely weaken particular trade unions, for example the Fire Brigades Union and the postal workers in the Communication Workers Union. It is no surprise that railway workers in the RMT and fire fighters in the FBU have in recent years taken votes to disaffiliate from the Labour Party.

Labour has become business friendly rather than trade union friendly. The gulf between the rich and poor in society has grown under the Labour governments of Blair and Brown.

This raises the question of whether the Labour Party is still the political voice of the trade union movement. At Labour Party conferences trade union leaders are often portrayed as the awkward cousins who keep making a nuisance of themselves by asking for this and that. There appears to be a gulf between the aims and aspirations of the trade unions and those of Labour. If this gap remains, the question of who represents trade unionists will grow.

It is difficult to see trade unionists of the likes of Mary Macarthur being parliamentary candidates for the Labour Party today. How many of today's prospective Labour Party candidates have spent years rushing up and down the country supporting, organising and leading workers to victory?

There is a need for workers to have a political organisation full of agitators and class fighters in order that they can raise the solidarity and provide the experience and leadership to win the struggles of the future.

The similarity between now and 1910 is striking. Trade unions then faced the prospect of either a hostile Conservative government or a lukewarm Liberal one. Today trade unions face the prospect of either a hostile Conservative government or a lukewarm (sometimes hostile) Labour government.

But if and when trade unions attempt to build a new political voice for the working class, it is important to learn the lessons of the past. Any such new organisation must put the interests of the class struggle first and foremost. For if elections are the most important feature of any new party, not only will the class struggle become secondary, but it could also be seen as a hindrance to the electoral machine. Even the best of militant trade unionists, like Mary Macarthur, have been misled because of the strategy of placing elections above all other activity.

The struggles ahead

The Edwardian period saw the rich grab an increasing share of the nation's wealth while wages for working people stagnated and then declined in real terms. This was the underlying discontent behind the years of the Great Unrest.

Today we see a very similar situation developing. Since 1979 Britain's wealth has increasingly become concentrated in the hands of the super-rich. In 2008 the richest 1 percent of earners in Britain took almost 15 percent of the total pre-tax income. In 1979 it stood at 6 percent. The richest 47,000 people in Britain today have a combined pre-tax income of around £37 billion a year.[2]

The recent banking crisis has exposed the multi-billion pound bonuses received by a relatively small number of bankers.

In contrast, the poorest 10 percent of earners in Britain saw their share of the nation's income fall from just 2 percent in 1997 to 1 percent in 2008.

For the last decade average real wages have only marginally improved and now there is pressure for workers to accept wage cuts on the false premise that it may save their jobs. Any apparent increase in consumption is usually the result of increased personal debt rather than increased wages.

While this situation does not automatically create a new Great Unrest, the parallels are easy to see.

The banking crisis that swept across the globe from the autumn of 2008 is having a profound impact. Trillions of pounds of government (taxpayers') money has been thrown at the banks to bail them out.

All three major political parties in Britain now talk about cuts, cuts and more cuts to end the public debt mountain caused by the bank bail-outs and the subsequent recession. Suddenly what was affordable is now unaffordable, whether it be the local swimming baths or library, funding the state pension or pensions for public sector workers. Ordinary working class people are expected to pay the price of the economic crisis.

The potential power of the working class through effective organisation is an immense power. The women chain makers' strike of 1910 is but a glimpse of that potential power to change society for the better.

People make history. The women chain makers of Cradley Heath made history. Mary Macarthur made history. What we do today makes the history of tomorrow.

APPENDIX

BELOW IS a reproduction of Mary Macarthur's election address:

FELLOW CITIZENS

At the request of the STOURBRIDGE DIVISIONAL LABOUR PARTY, I have decided to stand as candidate for this Division at the forthcoming Parliamentary Election.

My candidature is enclosed by the National Labour Party, and has the warm support of the National Federation of Women Workers.

I STAND FOR THE AIMS and OBJECTS OF THE LABOUR PARTY, with whose comprehensive programme you are doubtless familiar.

TO UNITE ALL WHO CONTRIBUTE TO THE HEALTH AND WELFARE OF THE WORLD BY HAND OR BRAIN, TO SECURE, NOT PRIVILEGES FOR ANY SECTION OR CLASS OF THE COMMUNITY, BUT A FULL SHARE OF THE GOOD THINGS OF LIFE, MATERIAL AND SPIRITUAL, FOR ALL.

I DO NOT APOLIGISE FOR MY SEX. It takes a man and a woman to make THE IDEAL HOME, and I believe that neither can build THE IDEAL WORLD without the help of the other. In the new Parliament, where laws affecting every household in the land will be framed, the point of view of THE MOTHER, AS WELL AS THE FATHER, should find expression.

If I am returned to the House of Commons, I shall try to voice in a special sense the aspirations of THE WOMEN WORKERS OF THIS LAND, to whose cause I have been privileged to devote my life, and who, in every industrial centre in the United Kingdom and Ireland, are voluntarily contributing their pennies to the expenses of my Candidature.

I shall also feel entitled to speak for the WOMAN WHOSE WORK NEVER ENDS—the woman in the home, who faces and solves a multitude of problems every day—the woman who has been too often neglected or forgotten by politicians, the mother of the children upon whom THE FUTURE PRIDE AND STRENGTH OF THE NATION DEPENDS.

At the same time, I shall not be deflected from my duties to my constituents, men and women. No legitimate grievance (individual or collective) which may be reported to me will remain unredressed, if it is humanly possible for me to get it rectified.

No reasonable request for any assistance within my power, as a Member of Parliament, and consistent with the principles for which I stand, will be refused.

MY FOURTEEN POINTS

1. A people's permanent peace.

There must be NO MORE WAR, and the policy laid down by President Wilson seems to me most likely to achieve this aim. The peace settlement must be based on justice and equity between the nations. There must be an end of secret diplomacy. I am opposed to the contemplated SITTING IN SECRET of the Peace Conference. Its meetings must take place in the FULL LIGHT OF DAY. THE VOICE OF LABOUR FROM ALL LANDS—and not only from the vanquished countries—must be heard, and its accredited representatives must have place at the Council Table of the Nations.

2. The end of conscription.

I will strive for the abolition, ROOT AND BRANCH, of Conscription, Military and Industrial, IN THIS AND ALL OTHER COUNTRIES.

3. Justice, not charity, for soldiers and sailors.

All disabled men are entitled to AN ADEQUATE PENSION based on the cost of living. NO WIDOW OR CHILD SHOULD LACK THE NECESSITIES OF LIFE. Allowances to all dependants must be substantially raised, having regard to their needs and to the sacrifices made by the breadwinner for the country. THERE MUST BE NO SUGGESTION OF CHARITY.

4. The speedy return of the fighting men.

Our soldiers and sailors want to get back to their homes and families. THEIR WIVES AND CHILDREN WANT THEM BACK. There must be no unnecessary delay. AMPLE ALLOWANCES MUST BE MADE FOR THE MEN AND THEIR FAMILIES until suitable work, at standard rates, is available.

5. The restoration of freedom.

I will fight for Free Speech—a Free Press—Free Trial—for Social, Economic and Political Freedom—for the Repeal of DORA [Defence of the Realm Act], and especially Clause 40D.

6. A living wage and no unemployment.

I hold that every worker is entitled to a wage sufficient to ensure not only the necessities, but the comforts of life. THE FEAR OF UNEMPLOYMENT MUST BE REMOVED once and for all, and suitable work provided for every willing worker.

7. A man's pay for a man's work.

It should be illegal to employ a woman on the same work as a man for less pay. The standard of life must not be lowered by unfair competition. THIS IS IN THE HIGHEST INTERESTS OF BOTH THE MEN AND THE WOMEN.

8. The redemption of pledges.

The promises made by the Government must be kept. They must not be regarded as mere scraps of paper, as in the past. Nothing has reflected more discredit on our Statesmen than their disregard of promises.

9. A million new homes.

The Housing Problems cannot wait. Local Authorities supported by grants in aid must be required to provide well planned and healthy houses AT REASONABLE RENTS, with every labour saving device, hot and cold water upstairs and downstairs, and plenty of cupboards. NO JERRY-BUILT DWELLINGS SHOULD BE TOLERATED.

RENTS MUST NOT BE UNFAIRLY INCREASED. The Rents Restrictions Act should be extended for two years.

10. Security for allotment holders.

The holders of allotments should be entitled to full (fruits and vegetables!) of their labours, and must not arbitrarily be dispossessed of the land which they have cultivated. In this as in everything else private interest must make way for public good.

11. The golden key.

The best education must be in the reach of all. There should be NO DISTINCTION OF SEX, CLASS OR WEALTH FROM THE NURSERY

SCHOOL TO THE UNIVERSITY. EVERY CHILD SHOULD HAVE AN EQUAL CHANCE. The financial problem for the parent must be solved by adequate maintenance grants. THE STATUS OF ALL TEACHERS, MEN AND WOMEN ALIKE, SHOULD BE RAISED. Their salaries, pensions, and training should be on a scale commensurate with the honoured place which they ought to hold in the community.

12. A fair system of taxation.

We shall have a war-debt of Seven Thousand Millions. Those who can best afford it must pay. I AM AGAINST ALL TAXES ON FOOD. The Income-Tax limit should be raised and further relief given in respect of family responsibilities. Super-Taxes and Death Duties should be increased. I am in favour of a Capital Levy exempting possessions under £1,000 and pressing lightly on possessions under £5,000.

13. Public good before private profit.

Land, Railways, Canals, Coal and Iron Mines, Life Assurance, Banking, Electricity and similar monopolies should be made public property, run FOR PUBLIC GOOD AND NOT PRIVATE PROFIT. Equitable compensation should be given to existing owners and shareholders.

14. The dignity of labour.

I believe in the Democratic Control of Industry. The workers should have a real share in management. Mere economic betterment is not enough. THEY ARE ENTITLED TO A FINER QUALITY AND TEXTURE OF LIFE, TO A NEW STATUS IN THE LAND.

I stand also for a MINISTRY OF HEALTH, the ABOLITION OF THE WORKHOUSE, INCREASED OLD AGE PENSIONS payable at 60, SELF GOVERNMENT FOR IRELAND, COMPLETE ADULT SUFFRAGE, THE ABOLITION OF THE HOUSE OF LORDS, the THE ABOLITION OF THE PRESENT CORRUPT HONOURS SYSTEM.

With regard to Temperance, I shall loyally support the policy of the Labour Party, which is to TRUST THE PEOPLE, by enabling each locality to make its own conditions as to the sale and consumption or prohibition of drink within its own boundaries, in accordance with the desires of the majority of the people in the locality.

It finds the KEY TO TEMPERANCE REFORM in the taking of the manufacture and retailing of alcoholic drinks out of the hands of those who find personal profit in promoting the utmost possible consumption.

In this, as all other social evils, I desire to get to the ROOT OF THE MATTER, and believe that the complete solution of this problem is bound up with the removal of bad social conditions generally.

THE ENGLAND WHICH SO MANY HAVE DIED FOR OUGHT TO BE WELL WORTH LIVING FOR. I desire to see it honoured among the nations for the Cleanliness and Beauty of its Cities, THE HAPPINESS AND HEALTH OF ITS CHILDREN, the Purity of its Politics and the Justice and Humanity of its Laws. I THEREFORE APPEAL TO THE ELECTORS OF THIS DIVISION, MEN AND WOMEN, TO SUPPORT THE IDEALS AND PURPOSE OF THE MOVEMENT WHOSE BANNER I AM PRIVILEGED TO CARRY.

Yours faithfully
Mary R Macarthur (Mrs W C Anderson)
Co-operative Rooms, Stourbridge
28th November, 1918

[Source: TUC Library Collection]